Little Pebble™

Staying Safe

Health Safety

by Sarah L. Schuette

Consultant: Shonette Doggett, coalition coordinator
Safe Kids Greater East Metro/St. Croix Valley
St. Paul, Minnesota

PEBBLE
a capstone imprint

Little Pebble is published by Pebble
1710 Roe Crest Drive
North Mankato, Minnesota 56003
www.mycapstone.com

Library of Congress Cataloging-in-Publication Data
Names: Schuette, Sarah L., 1976– author.
Title: Health safety / by Sarah L. Schuette.
Description: North Mankato, Minnesota : Pebble, 2020. | Series: Little pebble. Staying safe! | Includes bibliographical references and index. | Audience: Age 6–8. | Audience: K to Grade 3. Identifiers: LCCN 2018052362| ISBN 9781977108746 (hardcover) | ISBN 9781977110282 (pbk.) | ISBN 9781977108821 (ebook pdf) Subjects: LCSH: Health—Juvenile literature. | Health behavior—Juvenile literature. | Self-care, Health—Juvenile literature. Classification: LCC RA777 .S37 2020 | DDC 613—dc23
LC record available at https://lccn.loc.gov/2018052362

Editorial Credits

Erika L. Shores, editor; Heidi Thompson, designer; Morgan Walters, media researcher; Marcy Morin, scheduler; Tori Abraham, production specialist

Photo Credits

All photos by Capstone Studio/Karon Dubke

All internet sites appearing in back matter were available and accurate when this book was sent to press.

The author dedicates this book to her nephew, Wesley Hilgers.

Printed and bound in China.
001671

Table of Contents

Take Care

Take care of your body
and mind.

Stay healthy and safe.

Care for Your Body

Malik eats good food.

He wants a snack.

He chooses an apple.

Yum!

Sofia moves her body.

She jumps rope.

She takes a walk.

Yawn!

Lucas gets enough sleep.

He sleeps 10 hours at night.

A.J. stays safe from germs.

He washes his hands.

He uses soap.

Bao sneezes.

He coughs. He covers

his mouth with his arm.

He stays home when

he is sick.

Care for Your Mind

Feelings are important.

Ben talks to an adult he trusts.

Ben tells her how he feels.

Zack and his sister are mad.

He takes a big breath.

It calms him.

Healthy You

How do you care

for yourself?

21

Glossary

calm—to be quiet and peaceful; calm people think before they act

germs—small living things that cause sickness; washing your hands with soap kills germs

snack—a small amount of food; people often eat snacks between regular meals

trust—to believe that people will be honest and do what they say they're going to do

Read More

Chanko, Pamela. *Wash, Wash, Wash!* New York: Children's Press, 2018.

Clark, Rosalyn. *Feeling Angry.* Feelings Matter. Minneapolis: Lerner Publications, 2018.

Rustad, Martha E. H. *I Eat Well.* Healthy Me. North Mankato, MN: Capstone Press, 2017.

Internet Sites

KidsHealth: For Kids
https://kidshealth.org/en/kids/

Kids Healthy Eating Plate
www.hsph.harvard.edu/nutritionsource/kids-healthy-eating-plate/

Super-cool stuff!

Check out projects, games, and lots more at
www.capstonekids.com

Critical Thinking Questions

1. How can you stay safe from germs?

2. How can you calm down if you get mad?

3. What should you do if you sneeze or cough?

Index